REPORT

UPON THE

OYSTER RESOURCES

OF MARYLAND,

TO THE

GENERAL ASSEMBLY,

BY

HUNTER DAVIDSON, Esq.,

Com. State Oyster Police Force.

ANNAPOLIS:
WM. THOMPSON OF R., PRINTER.

1870.

REPORT.

STATE OF MARYLAND
STATE OYSTER POLICE FORCE,
October, 1869.

To the General Assembly of Maryland:

SIR:—I have the honor to submit the following report upon the Oyster resources of this State:

The Oyster in the Chesapeake exists in its native and uncultivated condition; none of the laws relating to it have provided any adequate means for its protection, but on the contrary, the general effect has been to open wide the door for its enemies, enabling us not only to predict its decrease, but its early destruction as an article of wholesale trade, in a few years, and the consequent loss of the direct public revenue therefrom.

This is the more to be regretted, as the peculiar adaptedness of the beds of the Chesapeake and its tributaries to the propagation and growth of the Oyster, and its wonderful natural increase, would, with ordinary care, supply us with a delightful and nutritious article of food at the cheapest rates, and insure a material increase of the public revenue for all time.

It is to be hoped, therefore, that our people will discard a serious consideration of those views, which it will be evident originate in local or individual interests, where they conflict with the general good in this matter, and permit the enactment of a law restraining and regulating the present thoughtless and improvident industry that takes every Oyster wherever found, regardless of season, size or condition.

It is well known that on the coast of France and England the Oyster had nearly been destroyed—becoming so rare as to disappear as an article of trade, and only to be found on the tables of the rich ; and this condition exists in England at the present; but in France, since 1869, owing to the investigations of the celebrated savant, M. Coste, the matter has been taken in hand by the Government, and wholesome laws enacted for the protection and cultivation of the Oyster, which has resulted in a bountiful supply, even for persons of limited means, and given employment to scores of thousands of poor dwellers upon the sea shores, who would otherwise be living in the utmost poverty and obscurity.

I regret that the laborious duties imposed upon the Oyster Police Force by the law, and the want of instruments, material, &c., have prevented me from making observations as to the extent and growth of our Oyster beds, to be embodied in the form of lithographic charts, with marginal notes for distribution to the counties; for I believe that this course—bringing the subject to the attention of the people, and giving them a comprehensive view of it—would go far towards reconciling the widely differing opinions I have heard expressed during the last two seasons, particularly in the tide water portions of the State, and which have caused me to fear the Oyster will be nearly destroyed before any legislation can be effected to remedy the evil.

In our waters there are two great interests in the Oyster trade, which have always been, and are likely to continue, at war, viz: the dredging and the tonging. The first has nearly all the means, and is backed by the wealthy packers. It has large vessels, well manned, equipped for heavy weather, and weeks of service off shore.

The latter class is represented by as many laborers, but is scattered in small boats that can only take the Bay in comparatively smooth weather ; in other words, the dredgers are strong and comparatively rich ; the tongmen are weak and poor ; and the worst of it is, that the former rarely lose an opportunity of impressing this fact upon the mind of the latter, by a too frequent transfer of the Oysters from the rich inshore beds--reserved by law to the tongmen—to the holds of their own vessels.

Any boundaries defined by law for the separate working of the two classes of Oystermen, must necessarily consist of imaginary lines, as the immense extent of our Oyster-beds would render it far too expensive to resort to buoys or artificial landmarks; but in neither case could the dredgers be kept from infringing the rights of the tongmen, unless the risk of punishment is made greater than the inducement to do so.

The ever-increasing demand for the Oyster, as an article of export, has so stimulated the trade in the Chesapeake, that the Oystermen will *risk* almost any weather, and overcome great opposition, to enable them to reach the handsome profits that are being offered them in the market; and a convincing evidence that their profits *are* great, is shown in the readiness with which these men pay their fines—ten thousand dollars having been imposed last season, and yet during the *first* month of this, one hundred and twenty-six *more* vessels are licensed than during the same month last season.

If, therefore, dredging is to be permitted, there is no way of doing justice to both these classes, unless after giving them ample opportunity to learn the law, such fines and other punishment shall be imposed as will make a violation of the law altogether too great a risk to incur.

In order to preserve our Oyster-beds as a permanent source of revenue, and to supply the reasonable demands of the market, I would earnestly recommend that dredging be restricted to the period from the first of November of one year, to the first of May of the next, and that the heaviest fines be imposed for dredging at night—say from sunset to sunrise.

It is warmly urged by persons who are interested in the *dredging* business, that that mode of taking the Oyster improves its condition, and increases the product of the beds. This *has been* true, though only to a very limited extent; but, as dredging is carried on *at present* in the waters of Maryland, quite the contrary effect is produced. Where the Oyster-beds are very thickly covered, and a latter year's growth is overlaying and choking that of a former, (as is seen in Virginia, but not in Maryland,) so that this process going on from year to year, is forming on the beds those conglomerate masses of shell and marine deposit termed Oyster rocks frequently rising from a depth of sixty feet of water to within a few feet of the surface, then to stop this process and, as a farmer would thin and weed his plants, use the dredge and spread the beds, giving more space to the Oysters to feed and develope themselves, is undoubtedly an advantage. But when this spreading and thinning has been done sufficiently, and we look at the other extreme, as in our waters, and find five hundred and sixty-three vessels, each having two dredges, that when filled weigh one hundred and fifty pounds each, making eleven hundred and twenty-six *harrows*, dragged by vessels, some of nearly sixty tons burthen, under full sail, over the beds night and day, without regard to the size or condition of the Oyster, we can readily see that the work is greatly overdone.

The Oyster is hermaphroditic, and each adult is said to generate about one million young a year, which is doubtless the truth. But the enemies of this delicious mollusk are so numerous and actively at work, that one in a million of the annual production does not come to maturity.

In the water, the star fish, the drill, the winkle, the crab, the drum fish, the sheepshead, the dog fish and the ray, during their season, subsist in a great measure upon the Oyster; but the unseasonable hand of man gives it no rest, and is greater than all other enemies combined.

The Oyster ejects its spat from April to about August, and the old Oyster, shells, and other congenial substances on the beds, soon become covered with young Oysters, the shells of which do not attain to sufficient size or strength to admit of handling, or other disturbance, until about the first of November; but the heavy *harrow-like* dredges commence dragging over the beds the first of September, and keep up until June, a grinding and attrition of a thousand Oysters to every one that is taken, thus crushing out the life of the young, filling up the open mouths of all with the bottom, covering them up, and turning and leaving them in every unnatural position.

The tongs or rakes have no such effect; they touch the beds in one small spot, gather on that spot alone, and bring up nearly all they touch, and, moreover, are not so heavy, or roughly used, as to crush or injure either the old or young Oyster.

It is not necessary, therefore, to restrict the labors of the tongmen, rather encourage them to the fullest extent, but it is worthy of serious consideration, if it is not well to give a year's notice that dredging shall cease in the waters of Maryland for *three years*, (the length of time the Oyster takes to come to maturity,) and let the market be supplied by the tongmen, which can easily be done, and without decreasing the revenue of the State except, perhaps, for the first year. In the meantime, the Oysters would be increasing with wonderful rapidity in the deep water not used by the tongmen, and at the expiration of the three years, let dredging be carried on to a limited extent, that is, confined to certain months, not exceeding six of the year, and regulated so as not to interfere with the tonging.

This would insure us a permanent trade and revenue, such as we have a right to expect from the great resources which nature has given us in the Chesapeake and its tributaries.

It would not do to stop dredging *suddenly*, as the material which those engaged in the business have provided would be thrown back upon their hands at a great loss, but the Legislature could pass a law this winter, limiting it to the months *between* October and May, for the following year, and after *that*, stop it altogether for three years.

Dredging at night, say from sunset to sunrise, should be punished severely, as there can be but a very limited protection, or cultivation, of the inshore Oyster-grounds, when constantly menaced by such an enemy at night.

When Oyster-beds have become reduced to a certain degree, in our waters, they will soon cease to produce at all, although the ground may be the most congenial for the purpose, as the crustacea, shell, and other fish, which prey upon them, will destroy the young as fast as they assume a tangible form, and many of the old will meet the same fate, and the rest die out. Therefore, where bedding is undertaken, the Oysters must either be well protected, or else sown in such quantities as to enable the increase to get ahead of the destruction.

Last season there were five hundred and sixty-three vessels licensed to dredge for Oysters, averaging twenty-three tons each, carrying about eight hundred bushels at a load, and making two loads a month to market for, say seven months of the year: summing up six million, three hundred and five thousand, six hundred bushels taken by the dredgers.

During the same period, there were nineteen hundred and seven canoes licensed, each taking about five bushels per day for twenty-six days of the month, and seven months of the year, making one million, seven hundred and thirty-five thousand, three hundred and seventy bushels taken by the tongmen, for sale, which with, say two million bushels taken during the season for "private use," will give an aggregate of about ten million bushels taken from the beds of Maryland annually.

These Oysters will average not less than thirty-five cents per bushel, which gives, in round numbers, three million, five hundred thousand dollars as the annual value of our Oyster product, from which the law only enables us to derive a revenue of about forty thousand dollars above expenses.

When the light expense of getting these Oysters to market, and the fact that they belong to the *whole* State, is considered, it appears strange that we should neglect so fair an opportunity of increasing our revenue. The price of a dredging license should be increased from three to five dollars per ton, of the vessel. Those engaged in the business can afford to pay it, all that is said to the contrary notwithstanding. If the increased price of a license, and the reduction of a dredging time, should drive any from the business, very well, let them go, the tongmen will take their places fast enough; the Oyster-beds will be improved by it; plenty of Oysters will get to market; the revenue will increase proportionably, and the people will be generally benefited.

Taking an average of all, we will say, the value of a dredging vessel is eight hundred dollars; pay of crew, seven hundred dollars; wear and tear, one hundred dollars; food and fuel, three hundred dollars; making nineteen hundred dollars expenses for the dredging season.

We have seen herein, that such a vessel will run about eleven thousand two hundred bushels to market a season, which, at the average price of thirty-five cents, is thirty-nine hundred and twenty dollars; leaving a profit of two thousand dollars to a man who is owner and master, after having paid for vessel and everything invested. This dredging business in the Chesapeake, where a comfortable anchorage can be resorted to in a few moments, when desired, is much more remunerative than that of the Cod and Mackerel catchers, who risk their lives and their all, and frequently lose them, afar off the coast of New England, for months, during the stormy season, and many nights anchored on the ocean, with the sea breaking over them from stem to stern. And surely, then, in Maryland a superior class of men cannot allege their hardships in the Oyster trade as a reason for not increasing the price of a license.

I would recommend that a tax be imposed on the *carrying trade*, both ashore and afloat. Virginia has long been collecting such a tax, thus almost doubling her revenue from Oysters.

I quote from her Inspector's regulations, under the law:

"All persons shipping or forwarding Oysters by any vessel impelled by steam, or by railroad, or by express companies, shall first pay to the nearest Inspector the tax of three cents per bushel on all Oysters so to be shipped or forwarded........................"

Fine for neglect of this regulation "not less than fifty nor more than five hundred dollars."

"Any person desiring to catch Oysters may, if he thinks proper, pay the sum of three dollars per ton on his vessel, for a license to carry Oysters for one year. Such license permits the party obtaining them to carry or send Oysters to any market in or out of the State, for twelve months, free of further charge on his said vessel."

"All persons engaged in packing, pickling or opening Oysters for sale or transportation, shall pay a tax of one cent per bushel on all Oysters bought or taken for that purpose."

These regulations are not only in accordance with the State statute, but they are constantly enforced by the Military Commander of the District at the point of the bayonet, which leads us to the conclusion that there can be no difference of opinion between the National and State Governments as to the constitutionality of those measures; but we should consider that a State cannot *prohibit* the public right of fishery and navigation, though it can *regulate* that right.

(The question is, in reference to the Oyster trade, where does regulation end and prohibition commence?)

If, however, we impose this tax, it is best that it should not exceed the moiety of the Virginia tax.

We are higher up the Bay than she is, and consequently farther from the Northern market by water. Our Oysters are not so salt and finely flavored, and do not command so high a price, and hence, we must offer an inducement in the *lower* tax for carriers to come to us.

Instances occur of vessels clearing from fifteen to seventeen *thousand* dollars on a *single trip* from our waters to New England, and yet they do not pay a mill more than the average of about thirty-five cents per bushel for their Oysters, to the vessels and boats that carry them alongside fresh from the beds.

As my duties do not permit me to interfere with the carrying trade, I have no means of ascertaining exactly what quantity of Oysters go directly out of the State; but as nearly as I can judge, it is about one-third of the product taken *for sale*, from which alone, with a tax of one and a-half cent per bushel, we would derive forty thousand dollars revenue, not including the expense of collecting it, which I am sure could be done for three thousand dollars.

Large quantities of our Oysters are being run out of the State by vessels which have gone through all the *forms* of law, and obtained licenses to dredge, but the owners of which are non-residents of the State. These vessels are made over for the *season* under false bills of sale; the parties *here* exhibiting to the Comptroller genuine Custom House papers, to obtain which they took an oath as *bona fide* owners, as they again do in the Comptroller's office, knowing at the same time that the vessels are to be run wholly in the interest of the real owners elsewhere, and rarely or never landing an Oyster in this State. Thus are our citizens crowded out of their employment, in which the law proposes to protect them, and the results of their labors greatly diminished.

The Oyster Law, as is now clearly and generally known, has very many defects; but no human mind could heretofore have seen what was necessary, in the conduct of this great trade, to protect the interests of the people in every respect.

The use of the dredge for upwards of fifty years has been the means of keeping afloat a class of sailors, who, from the free and roving habits of their lives, removed from the restraints of society, and even of the law, (until the Police Force was appointed,) have grown to think themselves masters of the Oyster situation, and the advantages and working of their trade have been kept to themselves by a tacit agreement, in order that they might reap all the profits without interference.

No reliable data could, therefore, be collected upon which to frame a law that would dispense justice to all, and satisfy the demands of the people at large, in this matter, until the means had been put afloat, under the authority of law, to obtain it.

It would be irrelevant, in this report, to show the particulars wherein the law *is* defective, or to suggest any changes in detail, but I have prepared notes thereon, which I will have the honor of submitting when required.

I will say, however, that the very nature of this business, conducted by such persons *afloat*, requires that a law more rigid in its provisions, and summary in enforcement, than laws are generally, be enacted as our Oyster Law.

Under almost any *Oyster* law there will arise cases of apparent contrariety, and often involving abstruse principles of law, as shown in the administration of the one in force, by the opinions of the Attorney General, and in the many appeal cases, in which the best legal talent of the State has been engaged.

Nearly all of these cases have first to go before the Justices of the Peace, whose total want of education, *in some instances*, renders them unable to comprehend a case, or pronounce an intelligent judgment.

It is, therefore, a matter for consideration, how to perfect such a law as we require, at the same time placing its enforcement in the hands of capable persons, who can be reached without causing unnecessary expense, in time and labor, to the State, or to the arrested parties in time, and the probable loss of perishable cargoes.

Some useful hints could be taken from the Virginia Oyster Law; it taxes the carrying trade, and collects more revenue than ours—seems to dispense justice, and is more concise.

But the advantages of requiring every vessel to pay for a license for the whole season's work, *before* taking or catching Oysters, as in this State, instead of paying a tax *per bushel* at the time of loading, as in Virginia, are shown, in practice, to be so much greater in every sense, as hardly to require discussion.

I think, contrary to the prediction of our earnest and experienced Comptroller in his last Annual Report, that he will give us a very favorable exhibit of the Oyster fund this year. Instead of the "expenses absorbing all the receipts," (which, of course, could not have meant the purchase of a steamer, as she is property, and paying a handsome interest, too, in the way of fines, &c.,) he will, doubtless, show a balance, over and above the entire cost of the steamer, and all the expenses of the State Oyster Police Force, of from fourteen to fifteen thousand dollars, for the fiscal year.

For the next year, having no purchases to make, the revenue will be increased by the amount of the purchases already made, and will also show an increase over former years, after deducting *all* the expenses of the State Oyster Police Force, even if the law remains as it is, and in this connection, it should be remembered that sections 33, 34, 35, 36, 37 and 38, of the law are inoperative, because there is no penalty for a refusal to permit the Oysters, sold in the city of Baltimore, to be measured, and in consequence about ten thousand dollars have been lost to the State Treasury, in the last two seasons.

The least estimate I have heard, of the quantity of Oysters sold in the city of Baltimore a season, is five million bushels, and if, as the present law intended, one cent per bushel is required to be paid, (by amending the above mentioned sections,) fifty thousand dollars can be collected from this source. Then, instead of requiring an unlimited number of measurers to take out *licenses*, let a proper number be appointed by the Governor, subject to the supervision of the Bureau of Labor and Agriculture, and to receive a certain proportion of what they collect, say one-half, which would pay ten reliable measurers—an amply sufficient number for the purpose—leaving the sum of twenty-five thousand dollars to the Treasury per annum.

It is impossible to execute any practical method of regulating the taking and trade of Oysters, without a force *afloat;* private rights, the maintenance of the peace, and even the majesty of the law, are but names without it. The State is entitled to a revenue from her Oysters, and the people demand protection in the trade thereof.

The present force cannot be reduced and be efficient; on the contrary, it cannot now do more than half the duty required of it.

The journals and books of record, regularly kept, will show the amount of duty performed, and are always open to, and shown, any citizen interested.

We have but one small, slow steamer, with which to visit twenty-five different Oyster localities scattered sometimes far apart, over tortuous routes, the extremes of which are one hundred miles from north to south, by seventy-five from east to west. I mention these facts *here*, because the people have been led to expect too much of this force, without considering the imperfections of the law under which it operates. It is expected to be in every locality at intervals of a few days, whereas about two months are required to make a complete tour of inspection, taking into account the time consumed by the average number of arrests and trials.

Those who are in the habit of violating the law, keep the run of our movements by a regular system of reports from one to the other, and thus are often enabled to escape punishment for their offenses; but because all is not done that is desired, is no evidence that the force is not necessary; it rather shows that the force should be increased to a proportion that will cover the field of duty.

To the first of October of this season, one hundred and forty-six cases have been tried before the Courts and Justices of the Peace by the Police Force, and ten thousand dollars fines have been imposed, which has materially modified the lawless operations of the Oystermen ; and, it is my opinion, that the patient consideration and attention which is due to every new enterprise, will in due time make this Force the means of developing our Oyster resources to an extent that will give the trade the highest rank in the market of the State.

The extent of our Oyster-beds is about three hundred and seventy-three square miles, ninety-two of which are closely covered, and the remainder scattering.

This field could be made to give profitable employment to twenty thousand laborers, in a few years from this, under the administration of proper laws.

The Oyster Grounds are divided nearly as follows:

LOCALITIES.	Square miles.	Remarks.
Swan Point, Kent county	6	Scattering.
Chester River	30	"
Sandy Point to Thomas Point, A. A. co.	11	"
Love Pt. to Kent Pt., Queen Anne's co.	8	"
Thomas' Pt. to Horse Shoe Pt., including S. and West Rivers, A. A. co.	20	10 Close. 10 Scattering
Eastern Bay and Miles River, including Poplar Island	50	Scattering.
Horse Shoe Pt. to Holland's P., A. A. co.	8	"
Holland's Pt. to the Patuxent, Cal. co.	8	"
The Choptank R., including Sharp's Island, and the outside of Tilghman's Island	30	"
The Hudson River, Dorchester county	15	Close.
From the Patuxent to the Potomac	8	Scattering.
From the Hudson River to Hooper's Straits, Dorchester county	10	"
Honga River and Hooper's Straits, Dorchester county	12	"
Fishing Bay, Dorchester county	10	"
Nanticoke River, Dorchester and Wicomico counties	14	"
Monie Bay and Wicomico River, Wicomico and Somerset counties	12	Close.
Holland's Straits, Dorchester county	7	Scattering.
Kedge's Straits, Somerset county	2	"
Manokin River, Somerset county	7	Close
Big and Little Annemessex Rivers, Somerset county	10	Scattering.
Tangier Sound, including Holland's Straits, Dorchester, Wicomico and Somerset counties	50	Close, but thin.
Potomac River and tributaries	20	
The Patuxent River	10	Scattering.
From Hooper's Straits to the Virginia line, on the Bay Shore	15	"
Total	373	

Number of Vessels and Canoes licensed in each county and Baltimore city, their tonnage, &c., during the season of 1868 *and* 1869.

COUNTIES.	Dredging Vessels.	Tonnage.	Tonging Canoes.
Queen Anne's	1	25	105
Talbot	....	....	246
Worcester	....	....	81
Kent	1	24	93
Anne Arundel	20	256	222
Somerset	238	4,726	246
Wicomico	12	143	110
Dorchester	46	1,316	257
Prince George's	1	42	
Charles	1	29	22
St. Mary's	2	32	336
Calvert	1	28	189
Baltimore city	240	6,039	
	563	12,660	1,907

The five hundred and sixty-three dredging vessels, last season, employed twenty-one hundred and seven white men, and fourteen hundred and fifty-three negroes. The canoes employed about thirty-three hundred and twenty-five in all, with the same proportion of white and negro labor; making a total of sixty-eight hundred and eighty-five men, independently of the labor employed in the carrying trade, which would probably swell the number to between nine and ten thousand hands employed *afloat* in the Oyster business.

The most liberal encouragement should be given to persons to plant and cultivate the Oyster. I know of no enterprise which is more remunerative, and which need give less anxiety as to certainty of results, if ordinary personal attention is given to the business.

Almost every bend of our shores, protected from the storms, is a little mine of wealth, if the efforts of our people can once be turned in that direction.

Few persons, not engaged in the trade, are aware how rapidly Oysters will increase in size and condition when taken from the native beds, the clusters separated, then culled and planted singly, and permitted to rest, undisturbed, for a season.

I know of an instance where fifteen thousand bushels were thus taken and treated, costing not exceeding fifty cents per bushel from first to last, and every bushel of which is now worth in the market one dollar and fifty cents. This is by no means an exceptional case, and is another strong argument in favor of restricting dredging, in order that labor and capital may seek this method of developing and giving a permanency to a trade now being destroyed, at the same time supplying the market with a superior and more remunerative article.

The approval, by the Hon. Commissioners of the State Oyster Police Force, of the Oyster boundary line between Maryland and Virginia, from Smith's Point to Cedar Straits, via the southern extremity of the Smith's Islands and "Horse Hammock," has settled all dispute between the Oystermen and the Police Forces of the two States, in that locality, as far as any boundary line could do so; and, also, has enabled the trade to pursue its peaceful course to the advantage of all interested.

Somerset county has enjoyed for many years, the exclusive privilege of *dredging* for Oysters within her own boundaries —the proceeds of the licenses being paid to her school fund. She has three-eighths of the whole dredging tonnage of the State, (as shown above,) and most of this turned loose for years on her water, to work *in any depth*, has so reduced the beds, that her Oystermen now exclaim, "Our Oysters are gone!"

The result is, that the Somerset men encroach upon the rights of the adjoining counties, and this has been going on for some time, creating such hard feelings as to lead to the habitual use of firearms on board the vessels and boats in Tangier Sound. The equity of the Somerset law is not very apparent: she has a law passed giving her the exclusive right to take, in a wholesale way, a large portion of the *State's Oysters*—and even the license *money* goes to her school fund; at the same time, her citizens can get license to dredge in any other waters of the State, not within the limits of any county.

She cannot claim these privileges on account of her large tonnage in the trade, as Baltimore has nearly a third more than she has, and must, of course, keep outside of *all* county lines; and the placing of this large tonnage in the trade, by a county, is not such an advantage to the State as to induce her to concede additional and exclusive privileges therefor, the *advantage* being rather in favor of the county. Nor can she claim them by reason of the Oyster product, within her boundaries, as she is rapidly exhausting it; moreover, the Oysters in the broad waters of the Tangier Sound can hardly be said to belong to *any county*, the boundaries of which are formed by distant marshes, having a dry spot here and there, settled by a very few fishermen.

I have felt it my duty to advert to this local Somerset law, because it occasions much dissatisfaction in the State, renders it very difficult for a police force to perform its duties in that vicinity, is exceptional, and hence, unjust in its provisions, and stands in the way of a general law that may develop this great trade to the advancement of the wealth and the influence of our State, in the scale of the nation. By reference to a map or chart, the relative Oyster interests of the three Tangier counties, and the evil effects of granting privileges to one county that are not granted to the others, *in the very same locality*, will be immediately understood.

Two methods are available as remedies:

First—Repeal the Somerset local law, leaving only the general law, under which *all* counties must carry on the trade alike.

Second—Repeal said local law, but grant its privileges to the three Tangier counties under the general law; which could reasonably be done in the one sense, that the Tangier waters of those counties are *widely separated* from all other counties of the State, controversies with which would not be likely to arise on this subject.

But as the matter stands, such legislative action should be taken as will place all the oystermen of the Tangier Sound under *one* law, thus reconciling conflicting interests, and guarding against the occurrence of violence and bloodshed, for the evil in that locality increases with every season.

I respectfully recommend that authority be given the Commander of this Force to enforce the laws relating to the fisheries, as well as the Oyster trade, so that the duties of the Force would be, the "Inspection of Fisheries," construed by law to include Oysters.

There seems to be a uniformity in this proposed system of administering the laws relating to matters *afloat*, through the agency of one office, that should commend itself to the consideration of the Legislature; in addition to which, full and reliable reports can be obtained for the State Government at all times, touching its water resources, and companies and individuals will feel a greater security in their investments in such enterprises.

Since 1820, upwards of thirty laws, relating to Oysters and the Fisheries, have passed the Legislature, and new forms and provisions have, from time to time, been adopted, evidently making an increased effort to meet the requirements of the occasion, but without avail, which may all be attributed to the one fact, that there was no force *afloat* to enforce the laws, and collect reliable and general information for the action of the Government.

The subject of the boundaries of the counties, (lying on the Chesapeake and its tributaries,) in connection with the Oyster Law, has been the cause of several long and earnestly contested cases in the Courts, and the Attorney General, also, has given the matter due consideration, and published his opinions thereon, which, with the decisions of the Courts, tend to show that the subject demands the earliest action of the Legislature, from the doubt and uncertainty that surround it.

It is quite evident that the laws relating to the Fisheries and Oysters cannot be perfected until the State and county boundary questions are definitely settled.

I have purposely refrained in this report from going into an investigation of the nature, growth and best method of cultivating the Oyster, or any scientific analysis of the subject, because I am quite sure, from my experience the past two years, that the trade having run far ahead of legislation, we have yet to take hold and regulate the matter as it is, gradually working ourselves out of existing difficulties, to a final development of these resources, upon a basis of increase and profit to our State, and her citizens individually.

I have the honor to be,
Very respectfully,
Your most obedient,

HUNTER DAVIDSON,
Com. State O. P. Force.

www.ingramcontent.com/pod-product-compliance
Lightning Source LLC
LaVergne TN
LVHW020636110826
845149LV00004B/1219

* 9 7 8 1 4 1 8 1 9 1 1 5 3 *